SIGHT WORDS

Written by **Shannon Keeley**

Illustrated by **Maru Jara**

FlashKids

This book belongs to

_____

Flash Kids
A Division of Barnes & Noble
122 Fifth Avenue
New York, NY 10011

ISBN: 978-1-4114-9908-9

Please submit all inquiries to FlashKids@bn.com

Printed and bound in China

Dear Parent,

Any time your child reads a text, more than half of the words he or she encounters are sight words. Often, these high-frequency words do not follow regular spelling rules and cannot be "sounded out." So, learning to immediately recognize these words "at sight" is a critical skill for fluent reading. This book covers 25 top sight words and includes lots of practice with tracing and writing, as well as fun word puzzles and games. To get the most from this book, follow these simple steps:

- Find a comfortable place where you and your child can work quietly together.
- Encourage your child to go at his or her own pace.
- Help your child sound out the letters and identify the pictures.
- Offer lots of praise and support.
- Let your child reward his or her work with the included stickers.
- Most of all, remember that learning should be fun! Take time to look at the pictures, laugh at the funny characters, and enjoy this special time spent together.

the

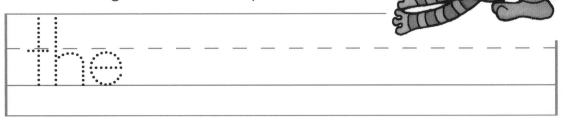

Practice writing the word **the**. Say the word aloud.

the

Write the word to complete the sentence.

The cat is on __ __ __ mat.

Word Find

The word **the** is hidden two times in each line.

Find the words and circle them.

e h t h e e t h t h e t

t e h e t h e e h t h e

and

Practice writing the word **and**. Say the word aloud.

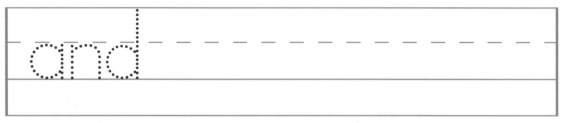

Write the word to complete the sentence.

Put on your coat ___ ___ ___ hat.

Rhyme Time

Circle the pictures that rhyme with **and**.
Underline the letters **a-n-d** in each rhyming word.

man

hand

sand

mad

a

Practice writing the word **a**. Say the word aloud.

Write the word to complete the sentence.

I have ___ bike.

Color the Pictures

Color the balloons that have the word **a**.

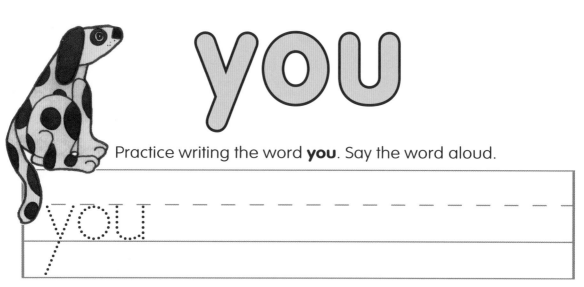

YOU

Practice writing the word **you**. Say the word aloud.

you

Write the word to complete the sentence.

He likes ___ ___ ___ .

Maze

Help the turtle solve the maze. Connect the letters to make **you**.

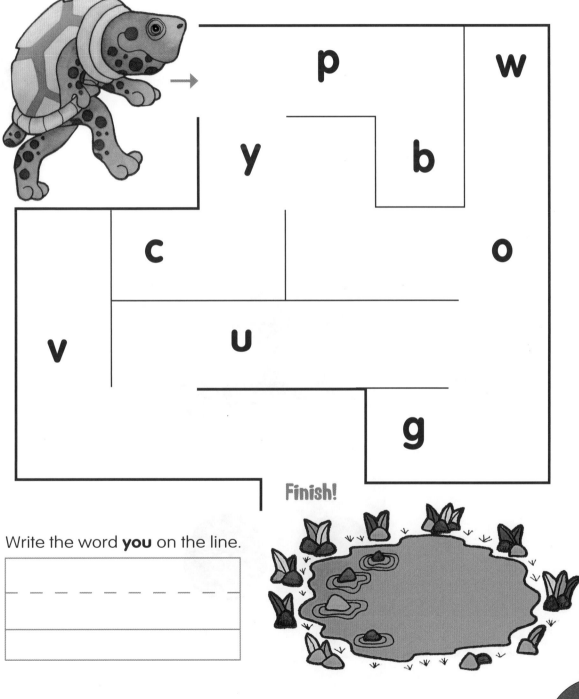

p   w

y   b

c   o

v   u

g

Finish!

Write the word **you** on the line.

of

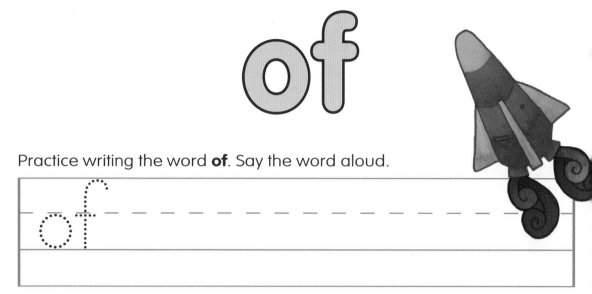

Practice writing the word **of**. Say the word aloud.

of

Write the word to complete the sentence.

I have a box ___ ___ toys.

Tic Tac Toe

Circle the row that has the word **of** three times.
Then write **of** three times on the line below.

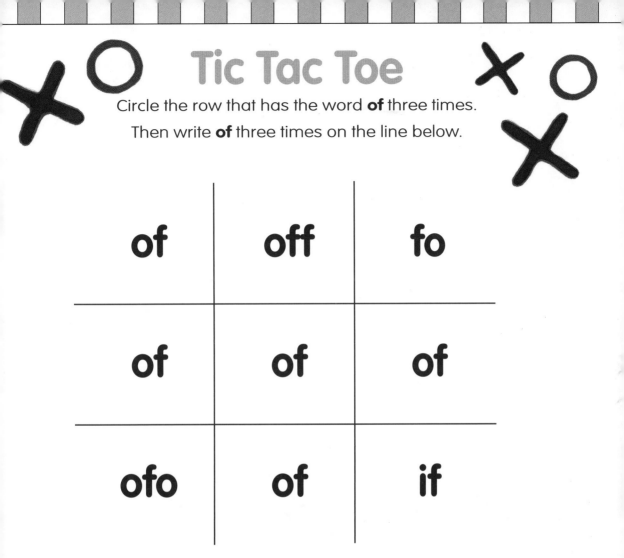

of	off	fo
of	of	of
ofo	of	if

Review: Word Search

Find the words in the word search.
Then write each word below.

the   and   a   you   of

y	t	o	u	a
o	h	e	f	d
u	a	n	d	n
t	h	e	h	y
o	d	u	o	e

Review: Story Time

Write the correct word to complete each sentence in the story.

the	and	a	you	of

Dear Friend,

I have something

for ___ ___ ___. It's ___ gift.

It's sweet ___ ___ ___

chewy. What is

___ ___ ___ gift?

A box ___ ___ cookies!

he

Practice writing the word **he**. Say the word aloud.

he

Write the word to complete the sentence.

Look, __ __ is my brother.

Word Find

The word **he** is hidden two times in each line.
Find the words and circle them.

e h e e h h e h t h c e

h e h h a h o h e h

it

Practice writing the word **it**. Say the word aloud.

Write the word to complete the sentence.

What is ___ ___ ?

Rhyme Time

Circle the pictures that rhyme with **it**.
Underline the letters **i-t** in each word.

sit

lift

lid

hit

I

Practice writing the word **I**. Say the word aloud.

Write the word to complete the sentence.

____ **like ice cream.**

Color the Pictures

Color the leaves that have the word **I**.

had

Practice writing the word **had**. Say the word aloud.

Write the word to complete the sentence.

I ___ ___ ___ a good time.

Maze

Help the bunny solve the maze. Connect the letters to make **had**.

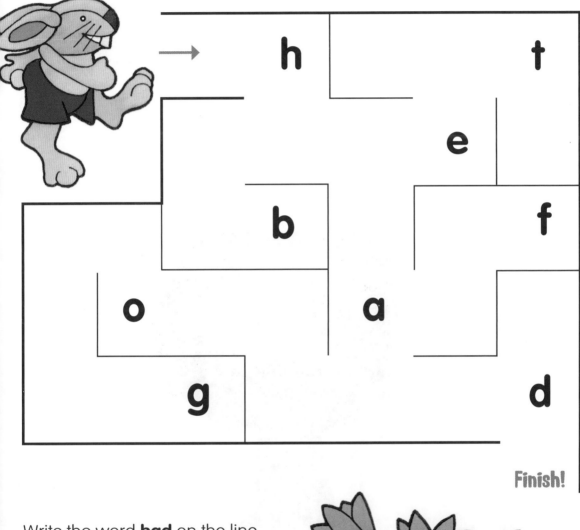

h   t

e

b   f

o   a

g   d

Finish!

Write the word **had** on the line.

we

Practice writing the word **we**. Say the word aloud.

we

Write the word to complete the sentence.

Today ____ ____ played.

Tic Tac Toe

Circle the row that has the word **we** three times.
Then write **we** three times on the line below.

we	me	we
ew	we	we
we	we	wee

Review: Word Search

Find the words in the word search. Then write each word below.

| he | it | I | had | we |

i	d	h	a	i
h	w	a	w	t
w	o	d	h	e
I	u	a	i	a
d	w	p	e	t

Review: Story Time

Write the correct word to complete each sentence in the story.

he	it	I	had	we

___ went to my brother's birthday party.

Yesterday, ___ ___ turned five years old,

and ___ ___ gave him a big cake. He

loved ___ ___ ! We ___ ___ ___ so much fun.

was

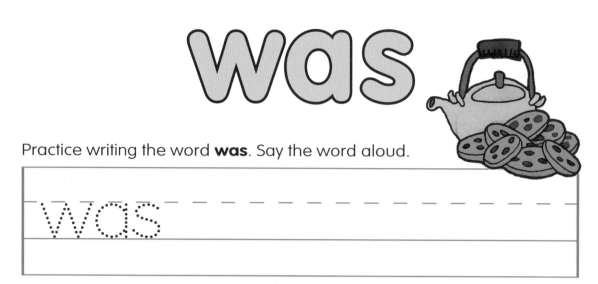

Practice writing the word **was**. Say the word aloud.

was

Write the word to complete the sentence.

The cookie ___ ___ ___ good.

Word Find

The word **was** is hidden two times in each line.

Find the words and circle them.

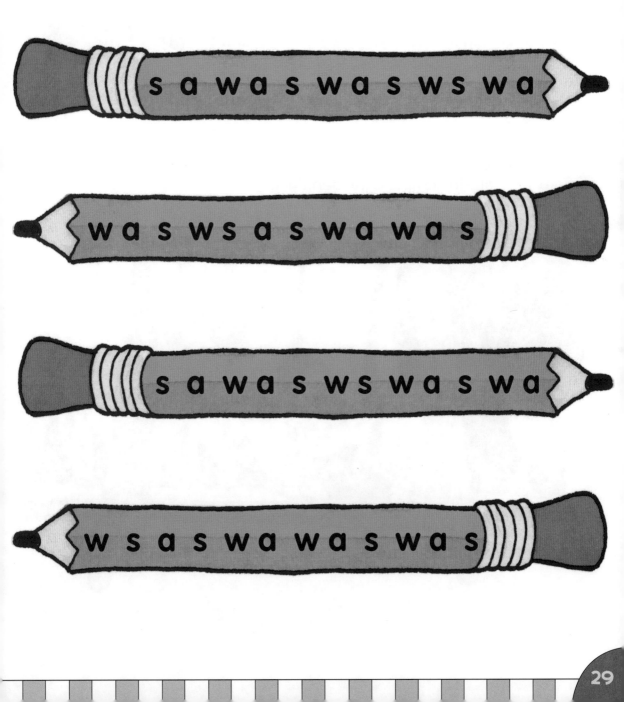

s a w a s w a s w s w a

w a s w s a s w a w a s

s a w a s w s w a s w a

w s a s w a w a s w a s

at

Practice writing the word **at**. Say the word aloud.

at

Write the word to complete the sentence.

I am ____ ____ the park.

Rhyme Time

Circle the pictures that rhyme with **at**.
Underline the letters **a-t** in each rhyming word.

cat

hat

dad

ant

she

Practice writing the word **she**. Say the word aloud.

she

Write the word to complete the sentence.

Where does ___ ___ ___ live?

Color the Pictures

Color the gumballs that have the word **she**.

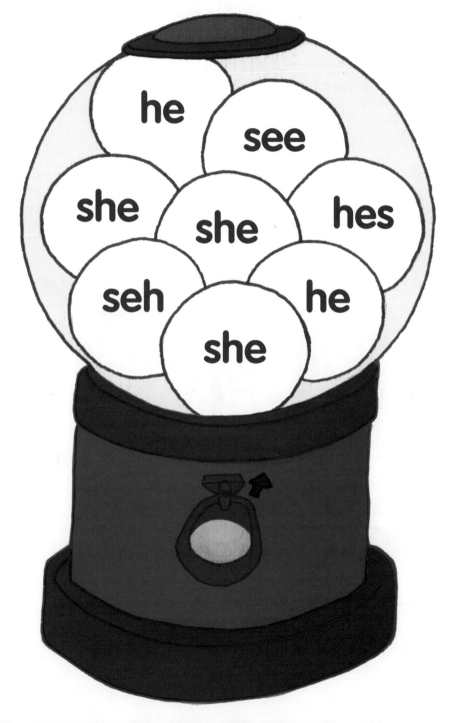

but

Practice writing the word **but**. Say the word aloud.

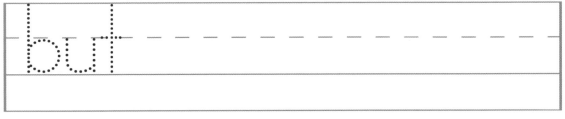

but

Write the word to complete the sentence.

I wanted to play outside, ___ ___ ___ it rained.

Maze

Help the pup solve the maze. Connect the letters to make **but**.

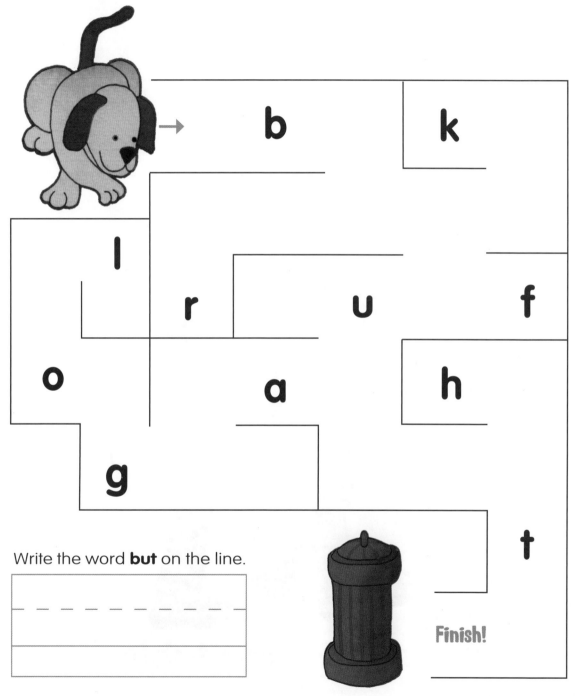

b

k

l

r

u

f

o

a

h

g

t

Write the word **but** on the line.

Finish!

on

Practice writing the word **on**. Say the word aloud.

Write the word to complete the sentence.

Put them __ __ the table.

Tic Tac Toe

Circle the row that has the word **on** three times.
Then write **on** three times on the lines below.

no	on	on
one	on	of
on	an	on

Review: Word Search

Find the words in the word search. Then write each word below.

was	at	she	but	on

b	u	w	a	t
a	w	s	h	u
o	a	s	o	t
n	s	h	e	o
w	b	u	t	b

Review: Story Time

Write the correct word to complete each sentence in the story.

was	she	on	at	but

It ___ ___ ___ a sunny day.

Anna and I were ___ ___ the park.

Anna said ___ ___ ___ wanted to swing,

___ ___ ___ the swings were broken.

So we played ___ ___ the slide.

to

Practice writing the word **to**. Say the word aloud.

to

Write the word to complete the sentence.

Let's go __ __ school.

Word Find

The word **to** is hidden two times in each line.
Find the words and circle them.

t t o o t o a t t f o t

o o t o o t t f t o o t

all

Practice writing the word **all**. Say the word aloud.

all

Write the word to complete the sentence.

Pick up ___ ___ ___ the candy.

Rhyme Time

Circle the pictures that rhyme with **all**.

Underline the letters **a-l-l** in each rhyming word.

nail

pal

fall

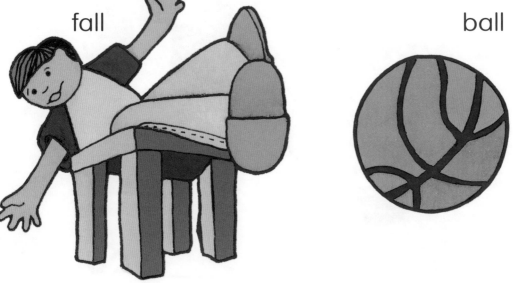

ball

for

Practice writing the word **for**. Say the word aloud.

Write the word to complete the sentence.

This gift is ___ ___ ___ you.

Color the Pictures

Color the rocks that have the word **for**.

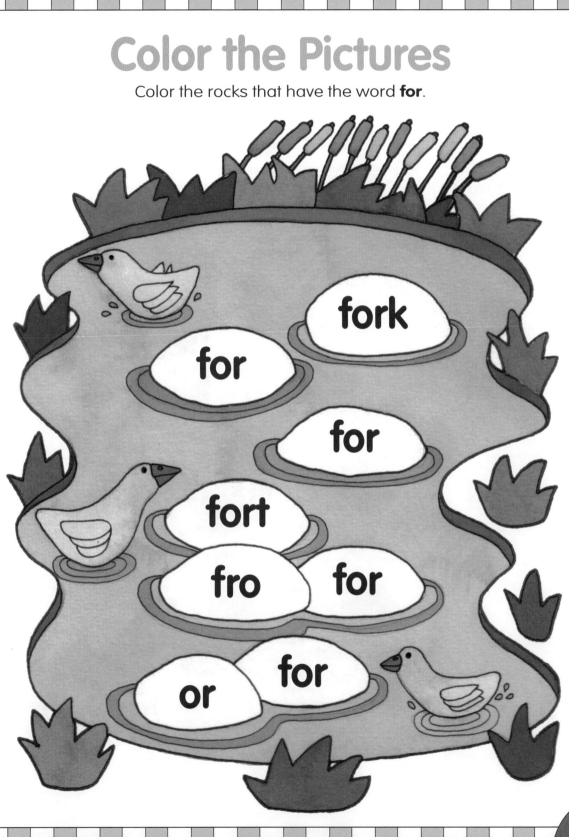

said

Practice writing the word **said**. Say the word aloud.

said

Write the word to complete the sentence.

Mom ___ ___ ___ ___ to wear a coat.

Maze

Help the cat solve the maze. Connect the letters to make **said**.

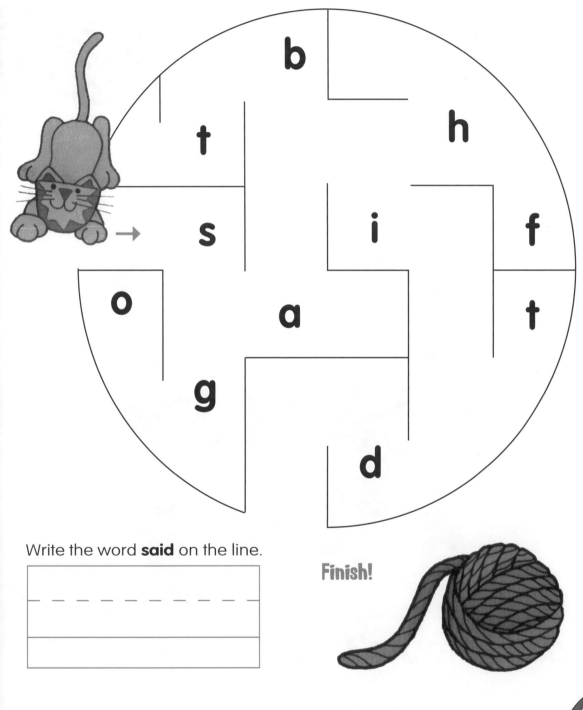

Write the word **said** on the line.

Finish!

they

Practice writing the word **they**. Say the word aloud.

they

Write the word to complete the sentence.

Are ___ ___ ___ ___ on the same team?

Tic Tac Toe

Circle the row that has the word **they** three times.
Then write **they** three times on the lines below.

they	they	hey
they	the	they
they	thy	they

Review: Word Search

Find the words in the word search. Then write each word below.

to	all	for	said	they

y	t	f	o	a
s	t	h	a	l
f	o	r	e	l
s	a	d	t	y
l	s	a	i	d

Review: Story Time

Write the correct word to complete each sentence in the story.

to	all	for	said	they

My family had a party ___ ___ ___ me.

___ ___ ___ ___ got a big cake,

and we went ___ ___ the park.

"Happy Birthday," they ___ ___ ___ ___.

I blew out ___ ___ ___ the candles.

SO

Practice writing the word **so**. Say the word aloud.

SO

Write the word to complete the sentence.

The water was ___ ___ cold.

Word Find

The word **so** is hidden two times on each sign.

Find the words and circle them.

s a o s o s o s

c o o s o s o s

o s s c o s

a o s o s o

in

Practice writing the word **in**. Say the word aloud.

i
n

Write the word to complete the sentence.

Get ___ ___ the tub!

Rhyme Time

Circle the pictures that rhyme with **in**.

Underline the letters **i-n** in the rhyming words.

on

fin

can

pin

with

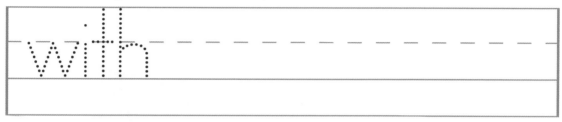

Practice writing the word **with**. Say the word aloud.

with

Write the word to complete the sentence.

I played ___ ___ ___ ___ my friends.

Color the Pictures

Color the fish that have the word **with**.

there

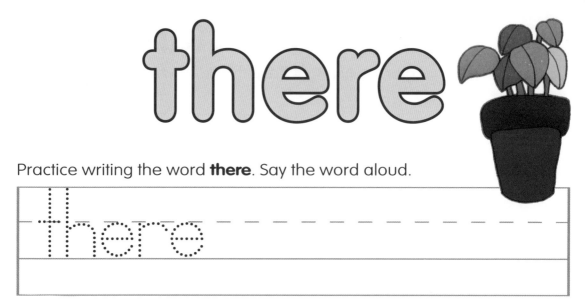

Practice writing the word **there**. Say the word aloud.

there

Write the word to complete the sentence.

My desk is over __ __ __ __ __ .

Maze

Help the bug solve the maze. Connect the letters to make **there**.

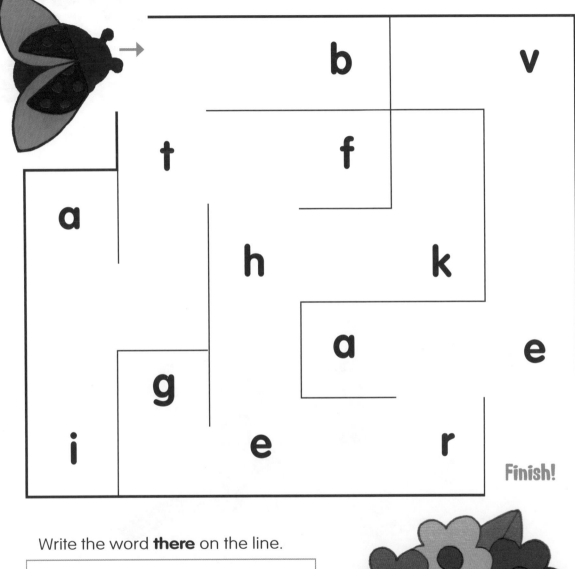

b   v

t   f

a

h   k

a   e

g

i   e   r

Finish!

Write the word **there** on the line.

can

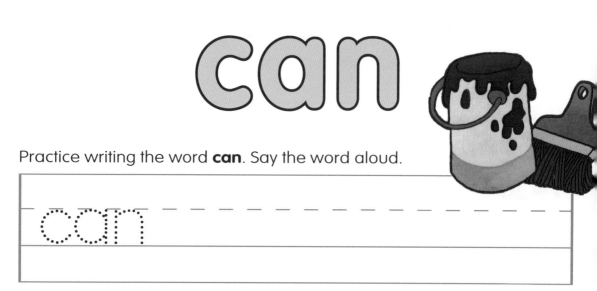

Practice writing the word **can**. Say the word aloud.

can

Write the word to complete the sentence.

I ___ ___ ___ help my mom.

Tic Tac Toe

Circle the row that has the word **can** three times.
Then write **can** three times on the lines below.

can	can	con
can't	cane	can
can	can	can

Review: Word Search

Find the words in the word search. Then write each word below.

so	in	with	there	can

t	h	w	i	t
a	n	i	o	h
c	o	t	i	e
r	a	h	n	r
s	o	n	r	e

Review: Story Time

Write the correct word to complete each sentence in the story.

so	in	with	there	can

"It's __ __ hot today," said Amy

"We __ __ __ go swimming," said Dad.

"Can my friend come __ __ __ __ us?"
asked Amy.

"Sure! Have her meet us __ __ __ __ __!"

"I can't wait to get __ __ the pool," said Amy.

Great job,

_____

(Name)

Now you know 25 sight words!